WINNING

the battles of

DESTINY

THE
CORNERSTONE
PUBLISHING

DR LADI OGABO

WINNING THE BATTLES OF DESTINY

Conquering the Foundational Strongholds

Copyright © 2016 by **Dr. Ladi Ogabo**

ISBN: 978-1-944652-20-3

Published by Cornerstone Publishing
A Division of Cornerstone Creativity Group LLC
  Info@thecornerstonepublishers.com
  www.thecornerstonepublishers.com
  516.547.4999

Ordering Information:

To order this book in bulk, please send email to Dr Ladi Ogabo: Pastorladi@gmail.com or call 407.517.8597.

Also Order online on www.amazon.com. Ebook version is available on Amazon Kindle.

FOREWORD

"According to the grace of God which is given unto me, as a wise masterbuilder, I have laid the foundation, and another buildeth thereon. But let every man take heed how he buildeth thereupon" (1 Corinthians 3:10).

When your foundation is sure, you can make a great edifice of your life. This is the main thrust of this book. Life is full of battles and everyone has his or her own fair share of them. But things get more complicated when the battles are foundational. Many are living in frustration today because they lack knowledge of either the source of their battles or the secret of victory. The good news however is that, for such, the revelation they need is right here!

Dr. Ladi Ogabo has written a landmark and an unprecedented book. I have known her far beyond the stories written in this book and of those moments that she wrote about. Her testimonies are solid and true. She is a woman of destiny with great impetus and the audacity to challenge you to keep moving towards your destiny. This is why you need to pay

3

close attention to the message of this book. It is a product of divine inspiration, seasoned with personal experiences, practical examples, scriptural references and unforgettable testimonies.

In this book, you will discover the power of a solid foundation and receive insight into why bondage persists in the life of many brothers. You will learn how to avoid self-inflicted destiny wounds. You will receive kingdom keys to pulling down strongholds that persist in your life. Finally, you will receive total and permanent deliverance, a fresh anointing and an impartation of wisdom to stay free. It is indeed an all-inclusive package that guarantees both uncommon revelation and unprecedented transformation.

If you can put to practice the fundamental truths in this book, your complete and continuous victory over the battles of destiny is sure. You will be who God wants you to be and you will possess your God-ordained position in life and in eternity.

Rev. Dr. Charles Ndifon

President, Christ Love Ministries International

Apostle, Kingdom Embassy International Churches

Senior Pastor, Kingdom Embassy, Johnston, Rhode Island

DEDICATION

This book is dedicated to my Heavenly Father, who has never failed me. To Christ, who redeemed and sustains me. And to the Holy Spirit, my friend and mentor.

ACKNOWLEDGMENTS

I would like to acknowledge my late parents, Ogabo Adoyi and Titi Amuta Ogabo; thank you for the love, stability and great life lessons you gave to all your children.

My gratitude goes to my spiritual parents, Apostle Charles and Rev. Donna Ndifon, for healing my emotional hurts, and for ordaining and empowering me with the mandate to minister the message of love with a demonstration of God's miraculous healing power to the hurting world.

Many thanks to Prophet Effa Emmanuel, Prophetess Victoria Michaels Jefferson, Apostle Everton Weeks, Pastor Tracey Weekes, Apostle Brad Elijah, Bassey Mbiotem and Pastor Robert Leiva.

To Dr. Daniel Olukoya (MFM Nigeria), I appreciate you, sir, for granting me personal access, for the weeks you ministered to me in 2004, and for introducing me to spiritual warfare. I also thank Pastors Bolaji Ojuri, Samuel Olatunde and Joseph Salami (MFM Lagos) for your prayers.

To Pastor W.F. Kumuyi (Deeper Christian Life Ministry, Nigeria), thank you sir for taking me through in-depth study of God's word.

I am grateful to Pastor Kayode Owolabi (London), in whose church I pioneered my ministry as a deaconess; and Pastors Ed and Deborah Keaton of Ridge Assembly (Florida) for my first window of opportunity in USA.

To Apostle Lorna Henry and Pastors Nadin and Kess Smith, thank you all for believing in my vision and supporting me in all the community revivals in Kissimmee, Orlando Florida.

Many thanks to Dr. Andrew Osakwe, Apostle Emmanuel Maiyaki, Pastor Abolaji Muyiwa Akinbo, Pastor Bukky Alabi, Pastor Rick Reeves (TV Producer), Rev. Celeste LoSardo, Prophet James Shrader, Evangelist Sunday Oguche, Dr. Paul Enenche, Pastor Becky Enenche, Apostle Mitchelle Kelly, Apostle Ada Hagh, Prophet Lawrence Oilema, Apostle Theo

Smith, Apostle Dilliana Gideon Powell, Dr. Candace House, Archbishop James Okewu, Rev. John Salifu, Apostle Mark Excel, Pastor Mrs Ann Excel, Apostle Uyi Abraham, Dr. David Philemon, Georgia Peters, Attorney Joseph N. DeBaise II, Corinne Baumgartner, Dr Carlton Davis, Apostle Theo and Mrs Smith, and Dr. Mike Murdock.

I appreciate Pastor Gbenga Showunmi and his team at Cornerstone Publishing, as well all others who labored to make this book a reality. I am winning because each of you has directly or indirectly blessed me in diverse ways.

CONTENTS

INTRODUCTION

The questions have often been asked: how many of the challenges in the life of a man are caused by sin? How many are mere trials of faith? And how many are orchestrated by witchcraft spirits, foundational yokes and generational curses? And most importantly, is freedom from generational curses possible? Can one live to fulfill their destiny on earth even when they have to contend with forces that are not only formidable and deep-rooted in one's foundations but are also bent on subjecting one to a lifetime of struggles?

Detailed answers are provided in this book to each of these questions through the revelations of the Holy Spirit. But let me give a quick answer to the last question now. Yes, you can be free from the chains of your foundations. You can be free from the forces that seek to limit or even truncate your destiny. You can dream again, live again and become all that God has destined you to be! Here's God's assurance to you on this: **"Even the captives of the mighty shall be taken away, and the prey of the terrible be delivered; for I will contend with him who contends with you..."** (Isaiah 49:25).

Let me also emphasize here that my purpose in writing this book is not to join any ongoing controversy or debate about generational curses, satanic afflictions or demonic manipulations. My mission here is to share with you what I have found out in my personal search for solution to life's challenges as an individual and as a pastor.

I have been engaged in many battles in my pursuit of destiny and purpose. I have been involved in all forms of aggressive prayer of faith from age seven. Fortunately for me, I realized early in life that focusing on Jesus and being purpose-driven is the only way to freedom from forces that exist to keep us in bondage. The plan of Satan and household wickedness was to put a limitation in every area of my life and cage me in Nigeria. But God elevated me to be educated in England and the United States, and He perfected His plans for me by prospering me in diverse ways.

Through the enabling grace of God, I have made

impact on schools and communities in London, UK, and Florida, USA. And still to the glory of God, I am currently an ordained pastor. Today, I am the founder and a presiding pastor at Gateway of Hope Global Ministries (Miracle Center) Kissimmee, Florida - where God is manifesting His miraculous power in numerous ways. However, this book is not about me. (I will be telling the full story of the wonders of God's grace in my life in another upcoming book). Rather, it was written to give you hope. It was written to inspire and empower every reader for a reawakening in their life and destiny.

Many have given up on their dreams because of the battles of life. But that's not God's desire for you. God's expectation is that you prosper and prevail in every area of your life. You are not a victim, you are a victor. You can be free to dream again. Maybe your past mistakes are the prison bars with which Satan has been keeping you from moving forward. As you read this book, the Spirit of God will show you the way to lasting freedom and victory.

It is time to stop searching for solutions in carnal places or even powerless, lifeless churches. It is time to take responsibility for your destiny. You can free yourself permanently from abusive relationship, depression, frustration, rejection, and all hindering forces of darkness in Jesus name. It is time for the champion in you to emerge. It is your season of breakthrough and jubilation. It is my earnest prayer that, as you read, the Holy Spirit will illuminate your mind, liberate your spirit and set you on the path of perpetual dominion over every enemy of your destiny.

HOW SOLID IS YOUR FOUNDATION?

How Solid Is Your Foundation?

"If the foundation be destroyed, what can the righteous do?" (Psalm 11:3)

I have found out that both believers and non-believers go through problems of life that sometimes defy human effort. These problems come in diverse ways. Family dysfunction. Rejection. Affliction. Drug addiction. Depression. Divorce. Poverty. Marital delay. Infertility. These are just few of the several negative experiences that have kept so many in search of freedom. And one truth I have equally discovered is that not everyone in search of freedom wears the signs on their countenance. As someone once said,

"A person does not have to be behind bars to be a prisoner."

Many today are prisoners even while being physically free on the streets. They put up the appearance of calmness while struggling with the raging, paralyzing storms within them. Bear in mind that prisons come in different forms. There's emotional prison, financial prison, marital prison, ministerial prison and so on. Regardless of the different forms of imprisonment, however, one characteristic is common to all, and that is LIMITATION. The movement and progress of the prisoner is limited to the confines of the prison. And as time goes on, he or she soon begins to feel a sense of helplessness as every attempt to succeed or break through in life continues to meet with a brick wall.

As strange as it may sound, even church leaders are not exempted from this bondage of generational yokes. There are cases of great men and women of God struggling to be free from one bondage or the other. In fact, many servants of God have lost the zeal to minister - having been buffeted for so long by satanic oppression - but they continue to limp on in ministry, simply because of the fear of failure or fear of people's opinion. The result, as should be expected, is a powerless ministry and a malnourished congregation.

But, perhaps, the most remarkable discovery I've made so far in this regard (through personal Bible study, research and experience) is that most of the challenges or issues caging many today have their roots in faulty foundations and generational curses.

Raging Controversy

Now, I'm not going to pretend not to know that a topic such as generational curses often generates controversy in Christian circles. Yes, I'm very much aware that many born again Christians don't believe a believer can be affected by curses of the bloodline or even demonic attacks. They allude to the fact that the blood that Christ shed on the cross has blotted out every curse that may affect the believer.

To be frank, I also believe in the redemptive and regenerative blood of Christ. I can attest to the efficacy of the blood because I also have benefitted from it and continue do so. But one fact that cannot be denied and one question that remains unanswered is, why are many genuine men and women of God today struggling to be free from the same afflictions that their unsaved parents or siblings suffered from? (I will go into details of this in the third chapter).

Of course, not all bondages and afflictions are

rooted in generational curses. Some problems are self-inflicted, through the choices we make and those we ignore. But the truth remains that there are individuals whose life's challenges just can't be traced to any personal decisions; individuals whose experiences defy all explanations other than the fact that what they are going through is not peculiar to them – others in their family tree bore or bear the same burden, making it a conspicuous trend in such a family.

So, What's in a Foundation?

I believe you will have a better understanding of the seriousness of the issue we are looking at here if you get a good grasp of the significance of a foundation. I believe that it is not in vain that the Scripture says that once a foundation is destroyed, even the righteous can be thrown into a state of perplexity and helplessness. The imagery here was obviously derived from that of a physical building. Every knowledgeable builder knows that the foundation of a building, though underground and consequently out of sight, is the most important part of that building. It determines not just the strength and stability but also the shape of the building. It is the foundation that will determine whether the building will be solid and durable. It will determine the type of building and purpose for which it can be used.

This is why professional builders often pay special attention to this part of a building. For example, divorce rate is very high today because of bad foundations. When a marriage is not based on love and the perfect will of God but on lusts, it has a bad foundation. When a marriage is based on manipulations or accidental pregnancy and couples are forced to marry as a result of the pregnancy, such marriage is built on a bad foundation. When a marriage is based on beauty, looks, money, or even ministry titles and charisma, the foundation is bad.

Unfortunately for many sisters, many good and God-fearing brothers may not have money. Unfortunately for many brothers, many beautiful women don't make good wives. Moreover, not being born again before choosing a husband or a wife is a bad foundation because the choice of husband or wife would be made randomly out of various men or women. These are some of the reasons why marriages do not survive life trials and challenges.

It is wise not to lay a bad foundation because it is difficult to get rid of. The foundation you form today becomes a generational one for years to come. In fact, I read somewhere of someone building just a patio and what he said about the amount of time he and his partners spent on the work was a real eye-opener for me. According to him, "If you add up the time we spent on this project, you'd get roughly 27 hours. But here's the crazy thing: 24 of those 27 hours were spent on the foundation. Only the last 3 hours were spent on the visible portion of the patio."

Explaining why this had to be done, he added, "You can have the most beautiful paving stone or the most eye-catching paint color, but in the end, they don't really mean anything if you don't put the right amount of time into the foundation." This shows clearly why we can't just dismiss the issue of foundation of our lives as some myth or fairytale.

Foundation, with regards to human beings, refers to our background and the experiences we have passed through that have brought us to where we are today. There are people whom, at birth, were dedicated to idols or demons through certain pagan-like rituals. I have heard of a village where the indigenes were required to bathe their newborns in a certain river in a part of the village. So strong was this rule that even if the children were born in foreign lands that were thousands of miles away from the village, such children must be brought for the ritual. Of course, anyone with spiritual insight would easily know that such children were simply being dedicated to the demons in the river which would in turn have controlling influence on the lives of the children, unless they obtained freedom in Christ.

There are some who were unwittingly given satanic names at birth. And in case you think there's nothing to a name, then you might quickly consider two cases in the Scripture – Ichabod and Jabez. The Bible narrates the circumstances surrounding Ichabod's birth and naming: **"And about the time of her death the woman that stood by her said unto her; fear not; for thou hast born a son; but she answered not, neither did she regard it. And she named the child Ichabod, saying, "The glory is departed from Israel because the ark of God had been taken. And because of her father in-law and her husband"** (1 Samuel 4:20-21).

Except some divine intervention occurs in his life, the life of Ichabod would definitely be a repeated cycle of problems. In fact, Ichabod started having problems right from the womb. At his birth, his father and his uncle died; the ark of God, which was the symbol of God's glory on Israel, was taken away by an enemy nation. And then his grandfather also died. His mother finally sealed his fate by wrapping up all these negative circumstances in a name and bestowing it upon the

23

child. Any deliverance minister or pastor that would help Ichabod would have to take a spiritual journey back to the day he was born.

That was exactly what Jabez did, when he realized the implication of his name. The Scripture says of his life **"...his mother called his name Jabez, saying, "Because I bore him in pain." And Jabez called on the God of Israel saying, "Oh, that You would bless me indeed, and enlarge my territory, that Your hand would be with me, and that You would keep me from evil, that I may not cause pain!" So God granted him what he requested."** (1 Chronicles 4:9-10).

This shows that names, just like words, have great power. They carry spiritual implications that may have negative impact on their bearers. If Jabez had not been serious enough to do something about his foundation, represented by his name, his life would have been far from honorable, as it was described in the first part of the passage. I think this also explains the reason God had to change some people's names Himself. Abraham and Jacob are quick examples.

Note, however, that this is not a reason for you to become paranoid about your name or your children's names – the blood of Jesus is potent enough to wipe off every negative force embedded in any name. Still, caution must be exercised in what we call ourselves, our children or even our businesses.

Power of a Solid Foundation

In any thing we do in life, whether physically or spiritually, there must be a good foundation. The Bible says even the church of God is built on the foundation of the Holy Spirit and through the apostles. Foundational problems, or problems that have their roots in the foundation, usually appear more powerful and difficult to correct than ordinary ones.

How exactly does one correct a foundational problem? Should one destroy the building to get to its foundation? It is for this reason that laying a sound foundation from the beginning is crucial. This is why the Bible, in its wisdom, prohibits so many things, which many people still practice - to their own peril.

Actually, as Jesus points out in the Scripture, the storms and adversities of life often attack both structures with solid foundations and those with sick foundations. The difference however is that a solid foundation built on Christ will always withstand these attacks because of its staying power; while the one with a weak foundation will crumble like a pack of cards.

The bottom-line is that the foundation of our lives has a tremendous impact on our lots in life - whether success or failure, progress or retrogression, victory or defeat; all other factors, such as hard work, intelligence and even luck are secondary.

I don't know if you have ever heard of the Leaning Tower of Pisa in Italy. If you haven't, then I suggest that you do a little research on it because the facts about it are quite fascinating. For now, though, let me give you a brief description of this popular tourist attraction because of its relevance to the power of foundation.

The tower is actually the freestanding bell tower of the cathedral of the Italian city of Pisa. It is known worldwide for its "unintended tilt." This is the fascinating part because the tower was originally designed to be beautiful and imposing (with a height of over 180ft). Unfortunately, the building had not been completed before it began to tilt, bit by bit, until it became known as the LEANING tower. As I write now, frantic efforts are still being made to save the splendid but sickly structure from total collapse. What was responsible for such abnormality? A faulty foundation!

There are multitudes of people today whose lives are like this perpetually leaning tower. Rather than standing tall and strong in all areas of their lives, they seem perpetually bent under the crushing weight of some invisible force. They live in constant frustration as they can't understand why everything they lay their hands on does not prosper in spite of their qualifications, hard work and experiences. Some wonder why they have so much difficulty breaking through financially or getting married in good time; while others wonder why their marriages and relationships continue to crash over trivial issues.

Some of these people wander from church to church, prayer houses to prayer houses, prayer mountain to mountain without success. The reason is because they are ignorant of the real source of their predicaments, which lies deeply in their foundation. The truth is that ancestral curses, covenants and occult practices have polluted the foundation of many innocent victims. Yes, as believers, our past is gone but that doesn't mean it is dead. Our tomorrow is what we make of our today.

Many lives, destinies, marriages, ministries, communities and even nations are in shambles today because of some foundational and generational problems. But I have good news for you, reader. No matter how messed up your foundation is, there is a gateway of hope in Jesus Christ. It does not matter how difficult or complicated your circumstances are today, there is a way out. It doesn't matter how much havoc the enemy thinks he has wreaked on your life, home or destiny, the REDEEMER is waiting with open arms to give you a brand new life! **He says, "The thief cometh not, but for to steal, and to kill, and to destroy: I am come that they might have life, and that they might have it more abundantly." And then He adds, "Come unto me, all ye that labour and are heavy laden, and I will give you rest"** (Matthew 11:28).

There's ABUNDANT LIFE in Christ. There is ABUNDANT REST in Him. All He wants you to do is quit struggling on your own. Bring yourself to Him, just as you are. He is a specialist in breaking yokes, lifting off burdens, healing wounds, clearing scars and making a masterpiece out of a complete mess!

If you want to stop the past from ruling your life, you must give your life totally to this Jesus. Be washed by the blood of Jesus, and be soaked in the word of God. You must be hungry for the baptism of the Holy Spirit. This is the only way to be set free.

ONLY GOD's divine intervention can free any man

from foundational bondage. No man or other power can free you. The great news for every believer is that as a born again and spirit-filled Christian, our true foundation is Christ. The faulty foundation of your childhood can be repaired. As you pray the prayer points in this book (as I will be showing you later on) with faith, Jesus will step into your life to rebuild every faulty foundation and release you from every foundational bondage.

2

SYMPTOMS OF A SICK FOUNDATION

Symptoms Of A Sick Foundation

So far, I have provided some glimpses into certain indicators of a life in bondage of generational problems or one that is under the captivity of destiny-hinderers. However, I would like to give further details on this so that you can get complete illumination and take full advantage of the liberation that has been made available to you in Christ Jesus.

To start with, if you observe a pattern of negative occurrences in your life, which you had observed or which had been reported in the lives of other members of your family, then watch it: a curse is most likely at work. For example, if your grandmother was divorced and the same thing happened to your mother and now your own marriage is in crisis, with all indications pointing to imminent collapse – then know that there is a curse still at work. What you must do is engage in spiritual warfare to save your marriage. Yes, you are a Christian and may even be an anointed man or woman of God, but you need to pray.

If you are an African, born into a polygamous home, or you are from a family where there is a lifestyle of promiscuity, or culture of not being legally married, then there's a serious problem with your foundation. If your parents, grandparents or yourself have ever been involved in occult practices or witchcraft or voodoo, then there is a cause for you to break loose from bad foundation. It does not matter if you are a believer, saved, sanctified and filled with the Holy Ghost – these are awesome – but until the Holy Ghost fireworks get into the roots of your life, you may never be free.

Apart from the points I have noted above, the following are other symptoms that should stir you up to getting total freedom through the liberating power in the name of Jesus:

- Emotional instability and hearing strange voices that other people can't hear

- Lack of interest or motivation to read or study your Bible, or to pray.

- Repeated cycle of failures, bad luck and misfortunes.

- You have nightmares, with people threatening you.

- You are constantly eating, swimming or having sexual intercourse in your dream.

- Thoughts pushing you where you don't want to go.

- Delayed marriage/marital problems.

- Feeling caged and frustrated/feeling suicidal.

- Uncontrollable anger and hatred.

- Poverty and perpetual struggles to achieve anything worthwhile.

- Repeated cycle of negative issues that is common to other family members.

- Confusion and lack of direction that has become a lifestyle.

There is Hope

Please note that as I have repeatedly mentioned in this book, the message here is a message of hope, not of doom. A sick foundation does not mean the end of life. With Jesus, THE FOUNDATION EXPERT, the sickest of foundations can be cured, if you seriously desire to be made whole.

I've shown you an example of someone who showed that he was truly desperate to break away from the chains of the past that threatened to subject him to a life of perpetual sorrow and limitations. That person was Jabez. Now, I want to show you the life of another man, Hezekiah.

The Bible tells us that Hezekiah had a desire to break away from his sick foundation and he took concrete steps and it was done. 2 Kings 18:4 says of Hezekiah, **"He removed the high places and brake the images, and cut down the groves, and brake in pieces the brazen serpent that Moses made: for until those days children of Isreal burn incense to it: and he called it Nehushtan"**

Hezekiah knew his father did not worship the living God. He knew he had a bad foundation but he refused to inherit that foundation. He opted for a different and better option. You too have the power today to reject every negative foundation. You don't need to inherit a bad foundation. You can make a firm decision to have a different destiny other than the one that seems to have been chosen for you by the forces of limitation.

Join These Conquerors

Some other examples of people in the Scriptures who chose not to be bound by the fetters of their foundations include Abraham who had an idolatrous background. He took a firm decision by listening to the call of God – the call to a life of freedom and dominion – and from then on, his destiny took a new dimension. He went on to become not only the wealthiest man of his time but one of the greatest men in history. He became a father of many nations and a source of blessing to the world.

The same call of God is coming to you today through the message of this book. You can have a better life, despite all that has happened to you or your parents. You can have a glorious destiny, despite all the negativity that has been said to you or predicted about you. It's not the voice or man that matters – it's the voice of God!

What about Jephthah who was conceived of an illicit relationship and had to be chased away by his siblings because he seemed to be accursed? That man went on to become a mighty man of valor through the help of the Almighty God, the destiny-changer. Jephthah refused to allow his life and destiny to be shaped by the illegitimacy of his birth or the opinions of others about him. In fact, his life became so glorious that the same people who had cast him away had to go beg him to help them when calamity threatened to destroy them (Judges 11) .

What do I say of Ruth and Rahab? These two women have had their names permanently stamped among the most blessed and most unforgettable women in the history of the world. Yet, looking at their foundations, they should have been consigned to the garbage bin of history instead. Why? Ruth was from Moab, an accursed nation which not only had a foundation that was unspeakably vile (incest) but also a history of enmity against God. Rahab, on the other hand, was not only from a nation that had been earmarked for destruction for its pagan practices but she herself was clearly described in the Scripture as a harlot (Joshua 2).

Yet, these two remarkable women took steps that transformed their lives and destinies forever. They chose to be different from others around them by rejecting what fate had in store for them and accepting what faith in God could grant them. And God never disappointed them. No one hears of Orpah (Ruth's peer) today, nor the other people that were in Jericho in Rahab's time. But what of these two women? You never can mention the lineage of Jesus Christ without mentioning them. The choices they made in rejecting their past and accepting God's offer of liberation got them disconnected from horrible foundations and got them permanently engrafted into the ancestry of Christ.

These people I have mentioned can be found in the Old Testament but does that mean a shift in destiny, from negative to positive, is meant for them alone? Not at all. Several examples come to mind in the New Testament as well, but let me just refer you to two that I consider particularly striking.

Do you remember the Samaritan woman Jesus met at the well (John 4)? Can you guess what would have become of her, had she not had that life-changing encounter with Jesus? I tell you, she would have had a most frustrating destiny. You know why? All her hopes of a joyful and fulfilled life were centered on men. And as should be expected, she continued to move from one frustrating relationship to the other, hoping in vain that she would one day meet the man that would give her the rest of mind and happiness she craved. Of course, seeing her desperation, the men continued to use her as they wished. But thank God, she came across the real person she needed in her life – JESUS! Otherwise, she, like many other women in history, would have died seeking solution and satisfaction in the wrong place.

From the day she met Jesus, a new dawn began for her. The joy she felt was so real, so sublime and so overwhelming that she, whom at the beginning of her conversation with Jesus was reluctant to give a little water to him, ended up leaving her entire water pot as she dashed back to the town to share the joy of her encounter. Nothing mattered to her anymore – she had finally found rest for her soul!

Her case was not too different from that of the possessed man of Gadara. In fact, his case should have been considered totally hopeless because his was not just a case of demonic oppression but demonic INVASION! He had thousands of demons living inside of him and messing up his life as they wished. So bad were things for him that he could no longer live among humans; he had to make his abode in a graveyard. Yet, Jesus sought him out – just as He is seeking to help you right now – and he became a different man entirely. It was said of him that when Christ had finished his work of reconstruction on his life, people that were around came to see what had

40

happened. Guess what they found? **"...the man, out of whom the devils were departed, sitting at the feet of Jesus, clothed, and in his right mind"** (Luke 8:35).

It's Your Turn

Now you know why I said there's hope for you. Regardless of how bad you might have thought your case was, I am sure by now you would readily agree that things are not as bad for you as they were for many of these people I have mentioned. Moreover, as at the time these people got their liberations, Christ had not even died and resurrected. Now your victory is even surer because Christ, by His death, has blotted out **"the handwriting of ordinances that was against us, which was contrary to us, and took it out of the way, nailing it to his cross"** (Colossians 2:14) Halleluiah, there is no reason to be bound by curses anymore!

Below is my personal confession as I write this book.

Jesus is the great architect and builder of my life. He has blotted out every foundational problem from my life. I am free, I am free. I am free, from any foundational problem that had ever limited me. Whom the Lord sets free is free indeed. I am free indeed.

Open your mouth and declare your own freedom or stand in the gap for someone. If you have a sick foundation, look up to Jesus, tap the power in Jesus Christ as all the people mentioned above did and you will never be the same again. Many who would have been destroyed because of bad foundations are living successfully today. Believe and trust God to cure your sick foundation and He will do it. Jesus never fails and He won't fail to deliver you. Renew your mind and refused to be a slave to your tradition and culture.

Knowing Your Place and Power in Christ

One of the truths about the believer's power in Christ is contained in John 1:12: **"But as many as received Him, to them gave He power to become the sons of God, even to them that believe on His name."** Sons of God who understand their authority and apply it can never be captives of Satan or his agents. Knowing who you are in Christ will enable you to position yourself to FIGHT for your life, marriage, family and business.

When you realize, for example, that as a son or daughter of the King of Kings, you should have dominion in every area of your life, then you wouldn't want to settle for a life of bondage or limitation. This is why you must diligently search the scriptures to know God's assurances concerning your life as His child. And you must be determined to see that these assurances become realities in your life and family. It is not just about confessing these promises and assurances, you must be fully convinced about them and live them out on a daily basis.

Let me also say something again about the power of faith. Martin Luther once said that "God our Father has made all things depend on faith so that whoever has faith will have everything, and whoever does not have faith will have nothing." Every promise of God concerning your freedom and victory as a child of God is dependable but it takes total faith in the power of the sacrifice made on the cross for you to be delivered from anything that is contrary to the purpose of God for your destiny.

The groundwork of your freedom has been accomplished by Christ. This was why He declared before His death, "It is finished". All that needs to be done to ensure you don't live a life of struggle and affliction has been done. Paul the Apostle giving further details on this accomplishment at Calvary said, **"Having disarmed principalities and powers, He made a public spectacle of them, triumphing over them in it"** (Colossians 2:15).

Christ has triumphed on your behalf. Of this you must be sure, even for your victory prayer to be effective. **"...for he who comes to God must believe that He is, and that He is a rewarder of those who diligently seek Him."** (Hebrews 11:6). Faith honors God and God honors faith. Regardless of all that may be happening to or around you, God expects you to firmly believe that He wants the best for you and that He has the power to defeat every contender with your destiny. **"For I know the thoughts that I think toward you, says the LORD, thoughts of peace and not of evil, to give you a future and a hope."** (Jeremiah 29:11).

Let this uplifting assurance constantly ring in your heart, without leaving room for Satan to overwhelm you with doubts and fears. There are believers who make positive claims and confessions about the promises God has made concerning them but within their heart they are full of fear of the unknown. And let me say this here. Even though steps have been taken to explain the reality of generational curses in this book, the goal, as I mentioned earlier, is not to dabble into demonology or engage in scaremongering. The goal is simply to expose this area of the enemy's attacks, **"lest Satan should take advantage of us; for we are not ignorant of his devices"** (2 Corinthians 2:11). And with your awareness of this device of the enemy, you are able to obtain absolute victory by your faith and warfare prayer.

So, the fact that you know about generational curses doesn't mean you should always fear or confess generational curses; rather, you should nullify generational curses (if there's any) with confessions and prayers of generational blessings. Renew your mind daily by constantly feeding your spirit with the declarations of God concerning your destiny. Walking in fear and talking about being under a curse every time shows disbelief in the accomplishment of Christ on the cross. Therefore, make it a priority to declare victory, not defeat on a daily basis; and also make it a duty to live in constant obedience to God's word.

This is the secret of victory. To know, to declare and to do. Apostle Paul said: **"For our gospel did not come to you in word only, but also in power, and in the Holy Spirit..."** (1 Thessalonians 1:5).

Before proceeding to the next chapter, please pause here to pray the following. (Note: These prayers may not make sense if you are new to warfare but they work; so pray).

1. I release Holy Ghost fire of God to the foundation of my life; every negative thing affecting me, roast in Jesus name.

2. I loose myself from any bondage that I may have inherited from my parents in the name of Jesus.

3. I release my name from all foundational problems in Jesus name.

4. Holy Ghost fire, destroy the roots of inherited problem affecting my ministry, marriage, finances and health, in the name of Jesus.

5. I am a child of Jesus; my foundation is in the blood of Jesus.

6. I am free today in Jesus name. Amen.

The reason we pray these types of prayers is because most problems that are resistant to normal prayers are rooted in the foundation. We have to therefore attack the foundation.

WHY BONDAGES PERSIST

Why Bondages Persist

"Christ has redeemed us from the curse of the law, having become a curse for us (for it is written, "Cursed is everyone who hangs on a tree")" (Galatian 3:13)

I promised earlier on to give special attention to one of the burning and most controversial questions in the mind of many Christians today. Are Christians really subject to generational curses or foundational problems? If Jesus has paid the price of our redemption, why should any believer still be under a curse or under the captivity of evil forces?

Actually, it is true that Christ has paid the price of the freedom of every believer. The purpose for which He came and sacrificed Himself on the cross was to destroy the works of the devil (1 John 3:8-9); but you also have a major role to play to enjoy this freedom package. This redemptive work of Christ may not manifest in your life unless you appropriate it by taking some vital steps.

So, in answering the question on why foundational problems persist in the lives of believers, let me break the answer into the following points:

First, there is the problem of spiritual ignorance which leads to unnecessary captivity. Let me make this easier for you to understand. There is a huge difference between being born into a kingdom and taking possession of that kingdom. In other words, you may be an heir but yet live like a slave because you either do not know your rights or you choose to allow your rights trampled upon.

Here is something interesting from the Scripture on this (and you may be surprised!): **"Now I say, That the heir, as long as he is a child, differeth nothing from a servant, though he be lord of all"** (Galatians 4:1). Much earlier, before the Spirit inspired Paul to pen those words to the Galatians, God had lamented about His chosen people through Prophet Isaiah, **"My people are destroyed for lack of knowledge..."** (Hosea 4:6).

That is the reality of the kingdom. In the first instance, you have an heir living the life of a servant because he is still immature. In the second instance, you find people, whom God Himself declared as His, suffering and in fact subjected to destruction because they chose to live in ignorance. How does this apply to you? Simple. If you are saved, you are born into the Kingdom of Light. But you must go on to take possession of what the Kingdom holds. That is how YOU experience the finished work of Christ.

The blood of Jesus is powerful against every work of Satan but unless it is used in spiritual warfare prayer, generational curses will not go away. That is why the word of God (which is the sword of the Spirit), as well as the name and blood of Jesus have been provided as warfare tools to pull down all foundational and generational strongholds hindering our progress.

While your being born again frees you from the power, guilt and condemnation of sin; it does not automatically free you from the shackles of your foundation. What it does instead is to empower and position you to break off these shackles with the weapons of victory that have been placed at your disposal. Your new status as a child of God authorizes you to use the name and blood of Jesus as a "certified banker's check" to cash your freedom.

But doesn't this require deliverance? You may ask. NO, it doesn't. it requires faith in Christ and faith in the price on the cross - for it is the cross that has already delivered you. I said NO to 'deliverance', because over-dependence on deliverance houses, churches and ministers has weakened the faith of many – turning them to seekers of miracles, rather than seekers of the God of the miracles!

I personally was seeking solution in different places to free myself and my late husband from foundational and generational problems. Marital instability and childlessness drove me to so many deliverance ministers and churches. I later found out that my going round deliverance churches, mountains and ministers would never bring the required solution. Why? It was not because the deliverance pastors were not anointed; I found out later in life that the issues militating against any marriage required both couple to engage in spiritual warfare to win the battles. Don't fight alone!

As I said, I was going from pastor to pastor, church to church, seeking the men of God with power;

but I was not seeking the direct intervention of the Christ working in the men and women of God. I was desperate for solutions and didn't know any better as a baby Christian. Thank God, I realized that I needed to find out words in the Bible for myself. I read about Joseph, Hannah, David, Daniel and how they survived in crises. I developed a winning mindset. I started studying further about what the Bible says about generational curses and generational blessings. I began to renew my mind as I found out things for myself. This leads us to the second reason many believers remain bound.

The mentality of bondage and generational curses. Many believers see no reason they should do better than they are doing at present. They consider themselves victims who were unfortunate enough to be born into a family plagued by satanic bondage. They forget what the Scripture says in 2 Corinthians 5:17 that **"all things become new" in Christ and as such they are not doomed to a life of limitation.**

Let me emphasize one thing clearly: ALL GENERATIONAL CURSES ARE TRACED TO ADAM. God's original plan for man was a trouble-free life. Adam had a great relationship with God; Adam and Eve were in Garden with all they needed. God gave Adam total dominion over everything. It was a life of ease, until Adam fell to sin and disobedience. Adam's disobedience brought the foundation of a future life of pain and toil to Adam's children and down to us in this generation. The Adamic sin was the foundation of all human generational curses. But God so loves us humans that He sent His son Jesus to reconcile man to His original plan for creating you and me.

The curse on Adam became the foundation of the generational curse of man today. But the good news is there is also a generational blessing. Jesus died on the cross and His blood made atonement for the Adamic sins. Jesus' blood erased the generational curse; so we are new creations in a new generation. Every Christian therefore needs to take responsibility and make a decision to surrender completely to Jesus. Everyone needs to renew their minds to free their thoughts and confessions from generational curses to generational blessings. People need to read the word in the Bible, believe the redemption promises and have a renewed mind.

It doesn't matter how many deliverance programs one attends. What matters most is the level of faith in action after attending those deliverance meetings. Faith in the cross, not man, is a must! We need to believe and have faith that Jesus has redeemed us from curses.

We need to stand on the word of Christ to renew our minds; to embrace the deliverance the blood of Jesus has obtained for us.

It bothers me why many believers continue to be lackadaisical in dealing with the evils of foundation or generational problems. Many choose to dismiss it with carelessness. Some believe these problems will just fly past them without any effect. They do not meditate on the word of God nor pray. If you don't pray or if you only pray sluggishly without concentrating, or believing, nothing will happen. But when you pray with aggressive faith, spend quality time in the word of God, and pray in tongues when you don't feel like praying or when you don't know what or how to pray - only then will you begin to get results and experience real freedom from generational or foundational bondages.

My point here is that the provision for your freedom having been made, it is now left for you to decide whether to take full advantage of it or not. If, for example, you had millions in the bank and refused to cash or claim it, you would not have money and you would be deprived of many good things of life. It is the same with the redemption package and the word of God that is available for you. But whether you want to apply these truths in your life is another thing. Even God commanded us to **"Ask and you**

shall receive" (Matthew 7:7). You must PUSH for your breakthrough to manifest. By PUSH here I mean Pray Until Something Happens!

Say this aloud: "It is time for me to enjoy the benefit of my salvation. No more limitations for I am bought with the blood of Jesus!"

The third factor I want to mention is the influence of household enemies. The Bible warns us of this: **"For the son dishonored the father, the daughter riseth up against her mother, the daughter in law against her mother in law; a man's enemies are the men of his house"** (Micah 7:6). Many people are going through series of health issues, problems in marriage, relationship, career and business because of foundational pursuers from their very own family. For many, the witchcraft attacks are foundational problems from their brothers, sisters, parents, relations and people that know them very well, which makes things even more complicated for them.

Now, there is a need for caution here. The message here is not to make you become suspicious of every member of your family. As a matter of fact, as I will be pointing out later in this chapter, your issues or problems may not be connected to your ancestors or family foes. The point I'm making however is that the devil can use people in your family if they open themselves to his demons. The presence of spirits of envy, jealousy, unforgiveness and bitterness in a family makes such family a breathing place for demonic and witchcraft attacks. Think of Joseph and his brothers The spirits of envy and bitterness made the brothers to almost kill Joseph before eventually deciding to sell him to a strange land.

Household enemies have pursued so many people before finally killing them. And the most dreadful fact here is that running away from the city or country of your birth in an attempt to be free from household enemy attack is never a solution. You may change location but as long as there is no engagement in spiritual warfare prayers, there cannot be freedom. Moreover, warfare prayer is not going to work for you if you are praying and focusing on human enemies, rather than the devil making use of them. As the Bible says in Ephesians 6:12, **"For we wrestle not against flesh and blood, but against principalities, against powers, against the rulers of the darkness of this world, against spiritual wickedness in high places"**.

To conquer household enemies, make Jesus's arm your shield and fortress. Get filled with the power of the Holy Spirit, the power from the third heaven. No power can withstand the power of God. Psalm 144:1 will become your confession **"Blessed be the Lord my strength, which teacheth my hands to war, and my fingers to fight."**

The Place of Polygamy in Generational Bondages

It is important that I specifically talk about this because of its peculiarity to where I come from. Polygamy is when a man is married to more than one woman. This tradition is a "cancer" seed that has been sown in most African families so many generations ago. The negative consequences of polygamy are numerous. It breeds envy, strife, competition, suspicion and witchcraft.

Unfortunately, Christianity has not completely wiped out polygamy in Nigeria and most parts of Africa. Most African born again Christians are in constant warfare to free themselves from the evils of polygamous family foundation. Many born again men and women of God have become victims of the seed of polygamy sown by their fathers. This has become a monster that is pursuing our Nigerian and other African men and women today.

Many African cultures allowed more than one wife. This practice has been in existence for generations.

With the coming of Christianity, many Africans are now electing to marry one wife. However, the generational scars of polygamy are very present today. Many African men find it difficult to remain faithful to their wives, even when they want to remain faithful. We see many men making wrong decisions in the Western world too. While the Africans have concubine or wives, the men in America and Europe have 'baby mamas' everywhere.

This is a generational or foundational reproach. We have so many dysfunctional marriages and relationship today because of how parents had lived their lives years ago. We see these men moving from one faulty and adulterous relationship to the other. The individual becomes spiritually blind and deaf, the person no longer sees anything wrong in this type of Casanova and promiscuous lifestyle. He becomes insensitive to the voice of God or that of man. Suddenly such an individual loses all his wealth to promiscuous women; and then poverty becomes his reward.

Sexual diseases may afflict such a man, too. In most cases, the careless lifestyle leads the individual to abandonment of vision and focus. Worse still, so many have died prematurely this way, without fulfilling the purpose for which God created them. They have gone to their graves without any of their dreams completed on earth. This will not be your story in Jesus name.

4

WATCHING AGAINST SELF-INFLICTED BONDAGES

WATCHING AGAINST SELF-INFLICTED BONDAGES

"Be not deceived; God is not mocked: for whatsoever a man soweth, that shall he also reap" (Galatians 6:7)

My focus thus far in explaining the reasons yokes and afflictions often persist in the lives of people of God has been mainly on those that the victims themselves might not have had the power to prevent. However, I must say that there are times when afflictions and attacks come upon people of God and hold them and their families captives because of their own carelessness and misdeeds that opened the way for the enemy to strike.

I need to point this out so we can sometimes look inwards, rather than thinking of our family line, in trying to locate the source of our afflictions. It is also to help us to be on our guard always against the attack of the enemy.

To start with, some afflictions in the lives of believers are results of past demonic covenants they had made before they met the Lord. So many people and families have been going through repeated cycles of financial problems, marital problems, health challenges and other forms of problems for decades. The parents see their children and grandchildren suffering or going through similar experiences they themselves went through in life. They have sought solutions in many places with no success. Nobody knows what is the cause or the solution of the problems that is visiting them to the 3rd or 4th generation.

Unknown to some of such families, strange covenants entered into, directly or indirectly, can pursue a person in life until death. Some individuals' lives have been contaminated from birth, while others were donated to idols at tender ages. However, there are those who also enter into demonic alliances as a result of youthful exuberance, desperation or wrong counsel. Except all these demonic contracts are broken, such individuals will be under constant pursuit. Many say they are born again, they may even be worship leaders, pastors or church workers, but if they have not broken all covenants they had with familiar spirits, idols or cults, they will always experience failure.

Anyone who suspects they are being hindered by evil covenants must seek help. Jesus will only help when there is a complete surrender to Him. However, if one claims to be born again but is still holding onto some idols, talisman, amulets, Ouija boards, magical books, horoscope, and so on, the evil covenants will still pursue the individual. There is a need to genuinely commit to Jesus, confess and break all strange covenants operating in individual's life and break them in Jesus name. This is why we read in Acts 19:18-20: **"And many that believed came, and confessed, and shewed their deeds. Many of them also which used curious arts brought their books together, and burned them before all men: and they counted the price of them, and found it fifty thousand pieces of silver. So mightily grew the word of God and prevailed."**

The word of God cannot prevail in your life, if you're still holding on tightly to the magic of the world.

The next reason freedom eludes many believers is their refusal to part with sin. Let's not deceive ourselves; as sin brought evil upon Adam and Eve and their offspring, so also does it do to anyone who dabbles in it today. We need to take responsibility for our shortcomings and stop blaming all our problems on past ancestors. Sin opens doors to demonic attack. Anyone who is not totally yielded to the will and ways of Christ is bound to be attacked by forces of darkness.

The wages of sin is spiritual and physical death, the Bible says (Romans 6:23). Sin is a very strong force that pursues human beings and no matter where you run to, your sin will catch up with you. John 5 tells a story about Jesus' encounter with a man that sin had caught up with and kept in bondage for 38 years. After Jesus had healed him, He warned him: **"Behold, thou art made whole: sin no more, lest a worse thing come upon thee"** (John 5:14).

In the eyes of God there is no small sin or big sin. God is a God of grace; but when His grace is taken for granted, an individual grieves His Spirit and begins to obey the voice of Satan. Some people receive instant punishment for their sins; but for others, God allows the cup of their iniquity to become full before visiting them. The devil is very crafty and many born again Christians are compromising God's standards and lust is becoming the norm in the churches today. We need to abstain from every appearance of evil. We need to ask God to forgive us our sins and also to excuse us from the sins of our parents to the fourth generation. May the blood of Jesus wash off all generational bondages in Jesus' name!

I will like to also caution here that even if you are, a born again minister, pastor, prophet or bishop, you need to pray, confess the word and keep renewing your mind daily. Your being born again is a way to get out of foundational problems. Getting born again is not the solution; it is only a way to the solution. When you become born again and you do not live a Christ-like lifestyle you are going back to the sin nature of Adam.

I must mention also that another reason problems persist in the lives of believers is the harvest of the wrong seeds they have sown in the past. Many, in the course of moving on with their lives, career, and relationship have moved into lifelong problems unconsciously. They have taken wrong steps or decisions that have resulted in this cycle of repeated problems. The Bible captures this scenario in Ecclesiastes 9:12: **"For man knoweth not his time; as the fishes that are taken in an evil net, and as the birds are caught in the snare; so are the sons of men snared in an evil time, when it falleth suddenly upon them."**

Whatever a person does in life must be rewarded, whether bad or good. This is the reason the Bible says: **"Be not deceived; God is not mocked; for whatever a man sowed, that shall he also reap"** (Galatians 6:7). God is a rewarder of deeds. We should be mindful of the choices we make today for they become seeds for the generations to come. Your decision and ways of living today will either prepare a good future for your children or a bad one for them.

We see a trend in some families where every male child must be imprisoned for drug or crime. We see that the pattern has been happening for three to four generations. People who are ignorant of generational curses or foundational issues may accept it as their luck. However, until this is spiritually broken, the seed of poor decisions that the great grandfather has sown will continue to hunt future male children born into the family. If the curse is not broken, by praying and claiming the redemptive power of the blood of Jesus, the pattern of imprisonment continues.

Other pattern in a family may be drunkenness, divorces, joblessness or poverty. Some of these came as a result of satanic doors that someone in the family line has opened for the attacks to reign in the family. The message here is that there are consequences for every actions we take, bad or good. God is a God of love but He is a God that hates disobedience and wickedness. He is a God of vengeance. God said His vengeance will be visited on the wicked ones and their children. **"The Lord is long suffering, and of great mercy forgiving iniquity and transgression, and by no means clearing the guilty, visiting the iniquity of the fathers upon the children unto the third and fourth generations"** (Numbers 14:18).

A person who is being pursued by God's vengeance cannot experience the peace of God. No prophet, herbalist, voodoo priest, pastor or deliverance minister can rescue the person from the wrath of God. The only way out is to **"Repent ye therefore, and be converted, that your sins may be blotted out, when the times of refreshing shall come from the presence of the Lord"** (Acts 3:19).

The last reason I will mention is disrespectful attitude towards God or things pertaining to God. Every person's behavior and attitude is capable of bringing blessings or curses into the individual's life without anybody cursing or blessing the person. Many church-goers have mistreated their pastors and have attracted curses on themselves. God says, **"Touch not mine anointed, and do my prophets no harm"** (1 Chronicles 16:22). Many, like Judas, who betrayed Jesus, are stealing from the church account. They bring curses on themselves. Many married couples have exposed their children to demonic attacks by their lifestyles. The couples that fight or live demonic lifestyle are sowing bad seeds that will hunt their children emotionally and spiritually for life. An individual who is a gambler, lazy and disorganized is inviting the spirit of poverty by this type of lifestyle.

Our behaviors and attitudes must be Christ-like. Our lives must be completely given to Jesus Christ. **"Therefore, if a man be in Christ, he is a new creature: old things are passed away; behold all things are become new."** (2 Corinthians 5:17). All Christians should be watchful and mindful of the things they do and how they socialize with those who hate Jesus Christ. Curses can be inherited automatically. A person can inherit treasures; so also can one inherit curses easily as in the case of Gehazi (2 Kings 5: 26-27).

5

PULLING DOWN
STRONGHOLDS THAT
HINDER PROGRESS

PULLING DOWN STRONGHOLDS THAT HINDER PROGRESS

"For though we walk in the flesh, we do not war after the flesh: (For the weapons of our warfare are not carnal, but mighty through God to the pulling down of strong holds;) Casting down imaginations, and every high thing that exalteth itself against the knowledge of God, and bringing into captivity every thought to the obedience of Christ" (2 Corinthians 10:3-5)

The dictionary defines stronghold as "a well-fortified place; a fortress"; or "a place that serves as the center of a group, as of militants". And I think both definitions rightly apply to what we are considering here. In whichever way you choose to define it – whether as a mightily fortified fortress or as a place that harbors a concentration of militant forces – a stronghold is a major barrier that must be demolished to step into the promised land of our God-ordained destiny.

In the book of Joshua, for instance, we find that "Jericho" was a stronghold hindering the Israelites from entering their promised land. There was a prophetic promised land to enter, but before the children of Israel could go into that land flowing with milk and honey, they had to pass through a well-fortified city known as Jericho. It took a lot of action of faith, obedience and warfare and Holy Ghost fireworks before the wall of Jericho fell down (Joshua 6).

There's something remarkable and instructive about the way the wall of Jericho was brought down. God specifically asked the children of Israel to march around the wall for seven days. If you are someone who questions everything, rationalizes everything, and can be quite skeptical, you may ask; "Did God not have the power to point to Jericho and make it fall in seconds?"

Well, He actually could have done so; after all, how long did it take Him to part the Red Sea and later close it up again? However, God adopted another strategy in the conquest of Jericho because He wanted to teach His people the act and principles of spiritual warfare. God wanted to teach His people how to discover the power inside them. God instructed the Israelites to go march around wall of Jericho for seven days, and on the seventh day when the priest sounded the trumpet, they should all shout. They did exactly as God had asked them, and the wall of Jericho came crumbling down.

Now, here is how this story applies to you and me. Our journey as Christians can be compared to the journey of the Israelites from a land of bondage to a land of abundance and freedom. Many of us today have personal "Jerichos" and you may even be passing through your own now. Examples of "Jerichos" are unexplained barrenness, delay in getting married, unhappy marriage, divorce, poverty, sickness and rejection by loved ones and many more. These things have come to steal your joy, destroy you and kill you, so that you will not fulfil your destiny and purpose in life. But they can never defeat you, if you don't let them.

My personal experience has shown that even though God has great plans and promises for your destiny, your prophetic word or promises will not just manifest until you do something. You must battle with opposing forces who are bent on frustrating God's will for your life. And since you may sometimes not know exactly where these forces are coming from, you need to establish, through the leading of the Spirit, the type of warfare prayers to do to ensure your prophetic promises come to pass.

Get this settled in your mind: warfare is a must; so you cannot be prayerless and expect your prophecies to come to pass. Christ Himself declares that **"Men ought ALWAYS to pray and not to faint"** (Luke 18:1); and He went on to illustrate what He means by using the story of the widow woman who remained persistent in her petition until she was avenged of the adversaries frustrating her life.

It is time for you too to say to yourself, "enough is enough", and begin to pull down all the obstacles stopping you from moving forward. There is power in your mouth. Speak to your mountains and obstacles. Shout and command them to move. Speak life and not defeat to yourself. Proverb 18:21 says, **"Death and life are in the power of the tongue: and they that love it shall eat the fruit thereof."**

War against the Strongman

This is part of the warfare you must engage in. A strongman is what the Bible calls **"the rulers of the darkness of this world"** (Ephesians 6:12). A strongman acts as a prison-warden of the devil that diverts and confiscates the blessings that are programmed for the lives of individuals, families, communities and nations. Without binding and paralyzing this strongman, it will be extremely difficult, if not impossible, to achieve anything meaningful in life or fulfill destiny.

Jesus spoke about the significance of dealing with the strongman in Matthew 12:29: **"Or else how can one enter into a strong man's house, and spoil his goods, except he first bind the strong man? and then he will spoil his house."**

Daniel's experience in the Bible gives us a clear illustration of what a strongman can do to one's blessings, unless one remains persistent in the secret place of warfare prayer. He had been praying, with fasting, for twenty-one days, before having an encounter with an angel that told him what had transpired from the first day he had started to pray: **"And, behold, an hand touched me, which set me upon my knees and upon the palms of my hands.**

And he said unto me, O Daniel, a man greatly beloved, understand the words that I speak unto thee, and stand upright: for unto thee am I now sent. And when he had spoken this word unto me, I stood trembling. Then said he unto me, Fear not, Daniel: for from the first day that thou didst set thine heart to understand, and to chasten thyself before thy God, thy words were heard, and I am come for thy words. But the prince of the kingdom of Persia withstood me one and twenty days..." (Daniel 10:11-13).

Thank God that Daniel understood the power of prevailing warfare prayer. Otherwise, he might have given up as some believers do today. Note this clearly: a strongman is not just called that in vain. It's because they are very stubborn and wicked, and would not give up easily. That is why you must pray until you prevail.

Pray without ceasing to paralyze the strongman hindering your health, finance, marriage, relationship, church, family. Pray with **Ephesians 6:2, Psalm 118, 1 John 4: 4, 5:4, and 2 Corinthians 10:4**. Unless specific praying is done, the problems will generally remain or try to hide. The Bible says that the habitation of the wicked is full of cruelty (Psalm 74:20). You can ask the Holy Spirit to guide you accordingly. Speak in tongues, for the Bible says, **"Likewise the Spirit also helpeth** our infirmities: for we know not what we should pray for as we ought: but the Spirit itself maketh intercession for us with groanings which cannot be uttered. And he that searcheth the hearts knoweth what is the mind of the Spirit, because he maketh intercession for the saints according to the will of God" (Romans 8:26-27)

Pray and personalize the following points for yourself and your family:

1. Holy Ghost fire, consume every strong man monitoring my ... (life, progress, family) in Jesus' name.

2. Holy Spirit shield my...from all evil and wickedness in Jesus' name.

3. Let the Blood fight all...in Jesus' name.

4. Let the true peace and love of God reign in my ...in Jesus' name.

5. We arrest in advance every spirit of strife and hate in my...in Jesus' name.

6. Let love reign in our hearts and actions towards each other in Jesus' name.

7. Oh Lord, destroy every strong man hindering our financial blessings in Jesus' name.

8. We receive rest from all mental, financial and relationship problems in Jesus' name.

9. Let the blood of Jesus wipe away every negative word, spirit of poverty, sickness and misfortune assigned against our destinies in Jesus' name.

10. I refuse to live in the flesh or in lust. (Pray in the spirit and cancel all negative things that steal peace from your life).

11. Let the blood of Jesus erase all the legal grounds the enemy has against my life, marriage and business in Jesus' name.

12. I close all doors open to enemies in my life with the blood of Jesus.

13. You strongman of mind destruction, be bound in Jesus' name!

14. You strongman of financial destruction, be bound in Jesus' name.

15. I command the evil power source in my place of birth to be destroyed completely in the name

of Jesus.

16. Every problem that came into my life by personal invitation, depart, in the name of Jesus.

17. Any problem that came into my life through my parents, depart, in the name of Jesus.

18. I release all my locked up blessings in Jesus' name.

19. Oh God of promotion, promote me beyond my wildest imagination in Jesus' name.

20. Let every arrow of witchcraft go back to the sender in Jesus' name.

21. Let the Kingdom Light come upon my life and let darkness get out in Jesus' name.

22. I rebuke all the spirits against the soundness of my mind in Jesus' name.

23. I possess the mind of Christ in Jesus' name.

24. I am more than a conqueror; I have victory in Jesus name.

25. Give thanks. Thank God for answered prayers and go and enjoy a life of victory and peace.

PRAYERS FOR PERMANENT FREEDOM FROM EVIL YOKES

Prayers For Permanent Freedom From Evil Yokes

"And it shall come to pass in that day, that his burden shall be taken away from off your shoulder, and his yoke from your neck, and the yoke shall be destroyed because of the anointing." (Isaiah 10:27)

This is a beautiful assurance from God to you, saying clearly that whatever yokes and burdens that had oppressed you or your loved ones, business or ministry can be broken. And I particularly like the fact that the assurance begins on a note of certainty, "And it shall come to pass..." May this be so in your life in Jesus' name!

I have heard some Bible commentators who think this promise is only referring to the deliverance of the Jews from the captivity of Babylon. Others interpret the verse to mean the redemption of believers from the tyranny of sin and Satan. I believe the passage has a much wider application. But the most important thing is to identify what the Holy Spirit, who is the best Bible interpreter, is saying directly to you as an individual and then apply it to your situation.

The reason many people have failed to claim or stand on Bible promises designed to set them free from bondages is that they have been too dependent on commentaries and people's interpretations of the Scriptures, rather than depending on the Holy Spirit. When you spend time in God's presence with hunger to get revelation, the Holy Spirit can speak something new from the same scripture. So, never allow yourself to be limited by someone else's revelation, no matter how great it sounds. If you do, then you make the power of the Holy Spirit static in your life. The Holy Spirit is a dynamic personality and He gives diverse gifts and revelations to people as He chooses.

On reflecting on Isaiah 10:27, I see the yokes and burden of poverty, sickness, barrenness, delay, oppressions and any forms of witchcraft, foundational or generational bondages being destroyed. Only believe the word of God, and pray without doubting the omnipotence of God. You can be free from all types of bondages if you can pray with aggressive faith. As Jesus said, **"If thou canst believe, all things are possible to him that believeth"** (Mark 9:23).

Visualize your answers and see pictures of victory, not defeat. Note also that the enormity of your challenge should determine the intensity of your prayer. If, for example, a particular yoke has remained in your life for more than five years, the amount of prayer effort, which you must apply, must be equally strong. The satanic yoke must be broken such that manifestations are non-existent.

Breaking Limiting Covenants

Isaiah 28:18 contains a powerful promise of God: **"And your covenant with death shall be disannulled, and your agreement with hell shall not stand"**

A covenant is a strong and binding agreement between two parties. A covenant is similar to a contract with specific terms of operation. There are many types of covenants but they all have one thing in common:

A covenant cannot be broken carelessly at the wish of any of the parties. When, for instance, God makes a covenant with us, He always keeps His word. When we keep the terms of our covenant, we are sure that God will fulfill His promise, no matter how long it takes.

In the case of Abraham, we are told, **"And when Abram was ninety years and nine years, the Lord appeared to Abram, and said unto him, I am the almighty God; walk before me, and be thou perfect. And I will make my covenant between me and thee, and will multiply thee exceedingly..."** God's covenant with Abraham still stands till today. Abraham was faithful to the terms of this covenant and God has continued to bless and multiply Abraham's descendants till this day.

However, what I've described so far is the nature of divine covenant. But there are other strange covenants that people enter into knowingly and unknowingly. Many have entered into satanic covenants because the devil promised to give them temporary benefits in return for their souls. In this age of technology, many have joined some associations and have been initiated into cults and anti-Christ covenants. Many have fallen victim or become prey to this satanic cult because they are seeking remedies in wrong places.

In some parts of the world, people seeking power to

prosper go to sleep at a cemetery for twenty-one days. However, the type of power from such a place will be nothing but an expressway to losing one's soul to the devil. In some parts of Africa, some pregnant women make covenant with Juju priests; in other places like Haiti and parts of America, people enter covenants with voodoo priests or psychics. While the baby in the womb may not be directly involved in the covenants, the agreement terms will be binding on him.

As I mentioned in the third chapter, so many unsettled lives today are as a result of these kinds of covenants. Many issues of today are results of the evil covenants our parents and grandparents had entered into on our behalf. We, as believers today really need to probe into our pasts and those of our parents. The fact that we have accepted Christ does not automatically annul this evil covenant. Why?, we all must specifically pray and break it and all generational covenants and curses. Look at what the Bible says about this:

"If they shall confess their iniquity, and the iniquity of their fathers, with trespass which they have trespassed against me, and that also they have walked contrary unto me. Then will I remember my covenant with Jacob, and also my covenant with Isaac, and also my covenant with Abraham will I remember; and I will remember the land" (Leviticus 26:40, 42).

My Journal of Personal Prayer for My Family Tree to the 10th Generation

I have resolved to destroy every generational curse or foundational issue lingering in any area of my life and ministry. I have conducted a personal research into my family tree to the 10th generation and I have used the word of God to destroy every generational curse or foundational problem fighting me. After going from church to church, deliverance ground to deliverance ground, I decided to read and research on how to put a FINAL STOP to the generational covenants working against my family members.

Below is my family tree and the prayers I personally prayed. This is just a personal guide; I believe the Holy Spirit will guide you more.

1 Ogabo Adoyi (My Dad)
2. Adoyi Abutu (My Granddad)
3 Abutu Okpeke
4. Okpeke Ake
5 Ake Ogwuche
6. Ogwuche Abah
7 Abah Amuche
8 Amuche Oko
9. Oko Amuch
10. Amuche Eyi

(It does not matter if you do not know names of everyone in your family tree. Just pray; it works!)

Read: **Leviticus 26:40, 42; Isaiah 10:27; Galatians 3:13; 2 Corinthians: 5:17**

My personal prayer points for destroying generational curses and foundational bondage are as follows:

1. Holy Ghost fire, locate my foundation up to Amuche Eyi (my 10th father) and destroy every negative curse that has been working against me (in ministry, marriage.)
2. I have the DNA of Jesus; so the blood of Jesus cleanses me from every generational curse.
3. I command every limitation from my foundation - be corrected by the resurrection blood of Jesus!
4. Let the blood of Jesus blot out my sins and every sin of my parents on both sides to the 10th generation in Jesus name.
5. Philippians 2:10 says at the name of Jesus every knee shall bow. Let every diabolical knee from my family line bow in Jesus name.
6. Galatians 3:13 says, that Christ has redeemed me and my entire family from the curse of the law; so every problem from my family line is canceled. Jesus has become a curse on the cross for me; so from today I am free from all generational curses.

7. My family and I are no longer under Adamic sin or any curse from my ancestors in Jesus name.

8. Every curse of sickness, barrenness, divorce, poverty is destroyed today by the blood of Jesus Christ.

9. I believe in the redemptive blood of Jesus. We are redeemed.

10. I have moved out of generational curses and I am walking in generational blessings in Jesus name in Jesus name.

11. The word of God said who the Lord sets free is free indeed (John 8:36); so I am free from all bondages by the blood of Jesus Christ. I declare generational blessings over myself, children, grandchildren, husband and family in Jesus name.

PRAYERS TO DESTROY EVIL YOKES

(Read and meditate on Psalm 2 and Isaiah 10:27; worship and praise God).

Prayers Points

1. I stand against any power waiting to hijack my prayers in Jesus' name.

2. I break every yoke of joblessness in Jesus name.

3. I break every shackle of limitation in the name of Jesus.

4. I cover myself, family, business with the blood

of Jesus.

5. Oh Lord, forgive me of any sin that will hinder my prayers.

6. I ask for forgiveness for all family sins to the 4th generations.

7. The blood of Jesus wipes out mark of failure from my life in Jesus' name

8. I anoint my eyes and ears with the blood of Jesus.

9. Holy Spirit exposes all secrets fighting me, my children and ......

10. Let the anointing of Holy Spirit destroy every yoke of stagnation, delay in my life in Jesus name

11. Blood of Jesus wipe out mark of failure and rejection from.......in Jesus' name.

12. Oh Lord, enlarge my coast and establish me and my family for your glory

13. Let the anointing to excel in my school, career, ministry, business, marriage fall on me in Jesus' name.

14. Oh Lord I will not serve my enemies, my enemies will bow before me.

15. I will not labor and another person inherit in Jesus' name

16. I remove every embargo placed on my marriage in Jesus' name

Believe God has answered your prayers. Have a generational-blessings mindset, declare blessings daily. Do not go back to sin that will open the door for a new curse in your life. What you do today is a seed for your next generation of children. Remain in christ and bring others to him.

ENCOUNTER WITH THE GOD OF MIRACLES

ENCOUNTER WITH THE GOD OF MIRACLES

G od's desire for all of His children is all-round prosperity. **"Beloved, I wish above all things that thou mayest prosper and be in health, even as thy soul prospereth"** (3 John 2).

Unfortunately, so many people are neither enjoying sound health nor living in financial and spiritual prosperity. As you look around, you find people, including believers, who are plagued with all manners of sicknesses, financial lack and spiritual poverty. And the immediate question that comes to mind is: Can God be unfaithful or are His promises no longer dependable? The answer is a resounding NO.

God is ever faithful. Whatever He says He will do, He will surely do. Examples in the scriptures and even in our contemporary times confirm this. The problem, however, is that we have an adversary, the devil, whose sole ambition in the world is **"to steal, and to kill, and to destroy"** (John 10:10). Still, the good news is that Jesus has come to give you abundant life. So, you have nothing to worry about. Whatever good thing that seems to be dead or dying in your life will be quickened by the life that Jesus offers.

Whatever Satan has stolen or destroyed in your family, career, finances and health can be restored to you in multiple folds by the power in the name of Jesus Christ. You can be healed from all afflictions of the enemy in the name of Jesus Christ. **"For this purpose the Son of God was manifested, that he might destroy the works of the devil"** *(*1 John 3:8).

Satan uses afflictions to hijack the destinies of people. The reason people are troubled with afflictions of the mind, body and soul is to distract them from their focus and dreams. Satan knows that while they are preoccupied with seeking solutions to their trials and traumas, their dreams and visions could easily be abandoned. This is why you must never give up on your dreams and aspirations because of the battles of life. God is still at work and miracles still happen.

If you are confronted with a sickness or affliction that seems too overwhelming to bear, then contact a minister of God with the grace to minister healing to you. And the God of miracle will heal you. The scripture says, **"Is any sick among you? let him call for the elders of the church; and let them pray over him...And the prayer of faith shall save the sick, and the Lord shall raise him up"** (James 5:14-15).

The love of Jesus is available to heal all manners of afflictions and set all free from captivity. I have seen diverse miracles on the street, on the phone and in our church at Gateway of Hope Global Ministries, Kissimmee, Florida. The blind see, the cripple walk, relationships are restored and diverse breakthroughs are experienced.

I believe you would like to know about some of these miracles because nothing boosts faith like hearing of the wonders of God's power. This was why Christ told the man He had just healed and who was desperate to follow Him about: **"Go home to your friends and tell them how much the Lord has done for you, and how he has had mercy on you"** (Mark 5:19).

It is for this reason that I will be devoting the rest of this book to recounting testimonies of some of the miracles experienced in our church. These testimonies are meant to give the sick hope of recovery. Besides, we are expected to share testimonies of God's miracles in our lives to glorify God and to encourage others to believe the word of God for salvation of souls, healing of mind and body.

Luke 17:11-18 contains the account of ten lepers who had been healed by Jesus. Surprisingly, only one leper came back to Jesus to give thanks. Moved with commendation for the man, Jesus said, **"Were not all ten cleansed? Where are the other nine? Has no one returned to give praise to God except this foreigner? Then He said to him, rise and go you are made whole."**

The leper that came back to praise God got complete wholeness, which is better than just being healed. So, in obedience to God's word and expectation to share good tidings of His miracle-working power, I am sharing some of the various ways God has used me to bring healing and freedom to those in captivity of sickness and affliction. So many miracles happen instantly and frequently in our ministry that I can only share a few that were recorded. I give God all the glory, for without Him, I can do nothing.

Expect a miracle as you read the following testimonies that various people had shared with me.

MIRACLES AND HEALINGS: REAL LIFE TESTIMONIES

Instant Restoration of Life to the Unconscious

With gratitude to God, we the Oilema's family really appreciate God for how he has used pastor Ladi Ogabo as a source of healing to the family. Prophet Lawrence Oilema was seriously ill and hospitalized. He could not eat, talk or do any other thing for himself for a week. One day, he was taken to the shower room to have his bath. While there, he fainted and became unconscious. Soon after, the Lord intervened by using pastor Ladi Ogabo, a family friend, to locate his servant on the sickbed through a phone call. With just a simple prayer of faith, the unconscious man was restored to life in good health.

God has really used pastor Ladi Ogabo as source of help and healings in different ways to the family. One Alechenu who was on the sickbed also received his healing through pastor Ladi Ogabo's prayers. Pastor, your faith really strengthened our faith in God the more, and we the Oilema's family pray that the Almighty God will rain more of his glory on you to everyone in the nations in JESUS name. AMEN."

—EMMANUEL .L., FROM NIGERIA.

Stage 4 Brain Cancer Shrinking and Inactive

On June 1st 2015, I was diagnosed with stage 4 glioblastoma. I had surgery on June 9th to remove it, but only part of it could be removed. On June 27th, I started a set of chemotherapy and radiation to kill the rest of it. These treatment protocols were considered the best in United States, according to medical experts. However, despite these treatments, the cancer kept growing – to the point that I was asked to have another surgery, which I refuse.

One I day, I was in my aunt's store when I saw a beautiful lady walking in. She presented herself as Pastor Ladi. She said miraculous healings often took place in her church and that she would like me to attend. After a few days, I decided to go to her church - which turned out to be a great decision. She taught me some words of God from the Bible and prayed for me, pouring holy oil on my head.

Later, on May 13th, I had an MRI that revealed that the cancer was not only shrinking but also inactive. I praise God for my healing. And I wanna thank Pastor Ladi. God bless! –

—MR JEAN, KISSIMMEE FLORIDA, USA

Heart and Vein Disease Cured!

Dear Pastor Ladi, first of all, I want to tell you that it was an honor and pleasure for me to meet you. Secondly I want to give glory to God on how He used you to pray for me. In 2011, my legs were diagnosed with chronic venous insufficiency, a severe case of vein disease that affected the main vein connected to my heart. My legs were most of the time in some kind of pain and swollen. When you prayed for my legs, I felt the power of God on me; and by the time I returned to the vein clinic the doctor confirmed that I no longer have any vein disease. To God be the glory. I thank God for your obedience when He prompted you to pray for me. May the Lord continue to prosper you in all that you do, increase you more and more, and crown this year for you in His goodness so that your paths will drip with fatness! (Psalm 65:11).

Bless You,

—PROPHETESS JENNIFER .A. CHICAGO U.S.A

Lump Disappeared

Blessings, Pastor Ladi. Last night at the "Arise in Strength" conference, I was healed under the powerful anointing that you ushered in the place through your obedience to GOD. When you began teaching and preaching about the issues that people go through, you spoke specifically to many of my situations. As you spoke on the woman with the issue of blood from Mark Chapter 5, I received my healing after I released my "issues." As you said, "Issues of people draining you, not accepting you, weighing you down until you cannot fulfill your purpose..." that was me. Last night by faith, I reached for the hem of JESUS' garment and you came to my area and grabbed the hem of mine. I knew that I was healed by the POWER of JESUS! GLORY!

I never told anyone, but I had a lump on my back for a little over a year. As the saints began to testify of the healing that they received in service as you told us to "Take your eyes off of you and put your eyes on JESUS" I felt a fluttering all over the area where the lump was located...The HOLY SPIRIT allowed me to feel my healing and told me that, I am healed. Glory to GOD! I thank GOD for your ministry of healing and miracles!

—PROPHETESS ILJ

Other Miracles

• I was a guest speaker at a house bible group in

Poinciana Florida. The Holy Spirit soon began to heal all that were sick. Mr. John who had been blind in one eye was healed instantly.

- A lady was also brought to my house with a long-term sickness and vision problem. She was healed of all, including the vision problems.

- After Bible study, one Friday night, I met a man on the street who had been paralyzed in one leg by a childhood sickness. The second leg too had been damaged in a car accident. Doctors had told him he would never walk again, but when I touched him that night, he stood up immediately and walked. We were all shocked at how quickly God got him out of the wheelchair!

- After counseling and prayer of faith, the marriage of Chris and her husband was restored miraculously.

There are several other testimonies of miracles happening on regular basis. Divine favor, financial breakthroughs, unmerited blessings, people getting jobs they never imagined and so on. All of which proves that the power of God has not changed. Indeed, **"Jesus Christ the same yesterday, and to day, and for ever"** (Hebrews 13:8).

I believe you have been blessed by these testimonies, in addition to other liberating revelations in this book. Expect your own miracles. You have had a miracle contact with this book and your life can never be the same. Dream Again. Your blessings are permanent in Jesus' name!

THE GREATEST PRAYER
OF A LIFETIME

The greatest prayer of a lifetime is to be reconnected back to God in a living relationship. Relationship is the basis for asking. You cannot pray to a God whom you don't know and who does not know you. God wants to be intimate with you. This type of relationship is available to each one of us when we sincerely repent of our sins, and ask God's forgiveness, and receive His Son, Jesus, as our personal Lord and Savior. If you have never surrendered your life to God, or if you have turned away from God and you want to return to Him, now is the time. God is waiting for you. His arms are open wide to receive you. Just pray this simple prayer right now:

O Lord, be merciful to me, a sinner. I realize that I am a sinner. I need a savior and you are my savior. I repent of every sin, every wrongdoing, and I ask for your forgiveness. I receive Jesus Christ, Your only begotten Son, as my Lord and my Savior. I believe that Jesus went to the cross for me and paid the price for my salvation, and now I receive Him into my heart. I declare that I am born again. I am a child of God. Old sins are gone, and I have a brand-new life in Christ in Jesus' name. Amen.

ABOUT DR LADI OGADO

Dr. Ladi Ogabo is the General Overseer of the Gateway Of Hope Global Ministries and The Gateway of Hope Foundation, with the headquarters in Kissimmee, Florida. She has had series of community revivals and conferences with utmost manifestations of God's power, miracles and healings.

Dr Ladi holds a degree in Language Arts from Ahmadu Bello University, Zaria, Nigeria. She furthered her studies at the Roehampton University and the University of London respectively. She obtained a masters degree in Interdisciplinary Studies in Curriculum and Instructions from National Louis University Chicago (Tampa Campus). She was later conferred with honorary doctorate in Divinity from GMOR Theological Institute of America (Midwest Region).

As a British educator, teachers' trainer, and curriculum coordinator, she was one of the nationally trained teachers to train other educators in implementing the National Literacy curriculum in schools when it was first adopted in Britain. She is a consultant specialist in literacy, a certified educator in Florida, who has made great impact on children and parents in Polk County and Osceola County schools.

NOTE

NOTE

NOTE